From Far and Wide

A CANADIAN CITIZENSHIP SCRAPBOOK

Jo Bannatyne-Cugnet · Illustrated by Song Nan Zhang

Tundra Books

Text copyright © 2000 by Jo Bannatyne-Cugnet
Illustrations copyright © 2000 by Song Nan Zhang

Published in Canada by Tundra Books, *McClelland & Stewart Young Readers*,
481 University Avenue, Toronto, Ontario M5G 2E9

Published in the United States by Tundra Books of Northern New York,
P.O. Box 1030, Plattsburgh, New York 12901

Library of Congress Catalog Number: 98-61844

Canadian Cataloguing in Publication Data

Bannatyne-Cugnet, Jo
    From far and wide: a Canadian citizenship scrapbook

ISBN 0-88776-443-6

1. Citizenship – Canada – Juvenile fiction. I. Zhang, Song Nan, 1942-   . II. Title.

PS8553.A587F76 2000   jC813'.54   C98-932833-3
PZ7.B2266Fr 2000

We acknowledge the support of the Canada Council for the Arts and the Ontario Arts Council for our publishing program.

We acknowledge the financial support of the Government of Canada through the Book Publishing Industry Development Program for our publishing activities.

Design by Ingrid Paulson

Printed and bound in Canada

1 2 3 4 5 6   05 04 03 02 01 00

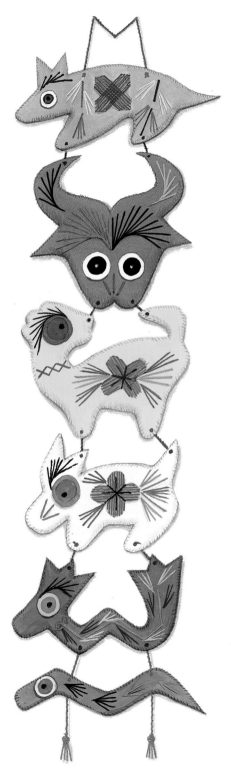

Dedicated to a fine Canadian, my son Tim.

J. B. C.

As proud Canadian citizens, my family and
I would like to dedicate this book, with love, to my
96-year-old father, who is still living in China.

S. N. Z.

My Canadian Citizenship Scrapbook

編文 李小玲
Written by Xiao Ling Li

攝影 丁 姨
Photos by Aunt T

艺术设计 李小玲
Art by Xiao Ling Li

For my new Canadian ~~sister~~ ~~brother~~ baby. I am making this book for you because you are not born yet and Mama says you will not get a citizenship ceremony like me. You will just be born Canadian.

On February 15th I became a Canadian citizen. So did Mama and Baba. My teacher, Ms. Fox, said our day was extra-special because it was also National Flag Day. This is the flag of Canada.

The day we became Canadians it was -22 degrees Celsius and snowing. Baba was outside first thing in the morning, when it was still dark. He had to shovel the driveway and clean the snow and ice off the car. He said, "I've waited four years for this day. We are not going to miss it because of snow." When it was time to leave, it was still snowing. We all helped to clean the snow off the car again.

I wore Canada colours to the citizenship ceremony. Aunt T gave me the red shoes. Aunt T says, "Red is a lucky colour, you know." She made sure Mama and Baba wore something red, too.

Welcome New Canadians

مرحبا بالكندي بين الجدد

歡 迎 加 拿 大 新 公 民 ！

Bien... nouveaux Canadiens

The citizenship ceremony was held at my school – Queen Elizabeth Elementary School on King Street. All the kids from my grade six class had special jobs. Megan and Raynelle met us at the door; Brett handed out programmes to people as they went into the gym.

Before I even got my coat off, Chelsea showed me a poster that said WELCOME NEW CANADIANS in Chinese. She made it just for me and said I could have it after the ceremony.

This poster says WELCOME NEW CANADIANS in French.

This is WELCOME NEW CANADIANS in Arabic. I think it is very pretty. I would like to learn how to write Arabic someday.

The front of the gym was decorated with thirteen flags of different nations. Mr. Quigley, the citizenship officer, told us that thirty-six people from thirteen countries were becoming Canadians at our ceremony. He showed us to our seats. He told everyone what to do. He explained stuff. He was nice.

e were in the second row, behind Sophia and Maria. They are twins. They are in kindergarten at Queen Elizabeth. Their parents had to escape from Ethiopia at night, or maybe be killed. The family came to Canada as refugees sponsored by a church.

The man beside me was Mr. Nguyen. Mama said he looked worried because his English was not so good. His wife and two boys became Canadians last year. Mr. Nguyen couldn't because he did not speak enough English or French. Baba told him, "Relax. You already passed the citizenship test. This is like a party."

But he still looked worried.

The gym got very crowded once the students and teachers filed in.

Aunt T was lucky to get a front-row seat. There were so many people with cameras, she had to stand in line to take pictures. Baba said the big cameras were for television. We were on the six o'clock news! The newspaper took pictures, too.

When everyone was in place, Mr. Quigley told us what would happen and what we were supposed to do. While we waited, Mama helped me write down all the countries the new Canadians came from on the front of the programme.

This is the coat of arms of Canada. I thought the lion stood for bravery and the unicorn for imagination. Mama said the lion stands for England and the unicorn stands for France.

These words are Latin. They say FROM SEA TO SEA. The crown reminds us of the Queen. I like the little lion holding the maple leaf.

"**O**rder in the court. All rise," said the Mountie, dressed in a red uniform.

Everyone stood up as the Canadian flag was brought in behind a girl playing the bagpipes very loudly. Baba joked to Mr. Nguyen, "I was wrong. One more test." He pretended to put his fingers in his ears. Mr. Nguyen smiled.

Once everyone was marched in, the Mountie said, "I declare this court open in the name of Her Majesty, Queen Elizabeth the Second, Queen of Canada."

Mr. Quigley introduced the man in the robe. His name was Dr. Williamson. He told us a story about how, over twenty years before, he had immigrated to

Canada from Scotland. He became a Canadian. He said he loved Canada and that Canada had given him its highest honour – the Order of Canada. He said we must all work hard for our new chosen country. He said our most important job is to be a good neighbour.

The ceremony was in both official languages of Canada – English and French. Our ceremony was special because it was in three languages. This is Ms. Singh, a teacher in my school, using sign language for the hearing-impaired students. I would like to learn how to sign someday.

The Oath of Citizenship

"I swear (or affirm) that I will be faithful and bear true allegiance to Her Majesty, Queen Elizabeth the Second, Queen of Canada, Her Heirs and Successors, and that I will faithfully observe the laws of Canada and fulfil my duties as a Canadian citizen."

«J'affirme solennellement que je serai fidèle et que je porterai sincère allégeance à Sa Majesté la Reine Elizabeth Deux, Reine du Canada, à ses héritiers et à ses successeurs, que j'observerai fidèlement les lois du Canada et que je remplirai loyalement mes obligations de citoyen canadien.»

 took my Oath of Citizenship in both English and French. I held my hands to my heart. Some of the new Canadians put their hands on a holy book.

We were called up by Mr. Quigley to get our citizenship certificates.

When Dr. Williamson gave me my Canadian papers, he said, "Welcome into the Canadian family." I said, "Thank you."

It seemed like I shook hands with a hundred people.

Mr. Nguyen had a big smile after he got his papers. When he sat down, he said to Baba, "Now we are safe."

Dr. Williamson threw his arms around the last woman in the line and gave her a big hug. I did not understand why he did this. When everyone was back in their seats, he asked our forgiveness for his excitement. He told us that the last new Canadian he congratulated was his wife! She was from Greenland. Everyone clapped for them. I cut their picture from the newspaper.

The school choir sang two songs. Mama cried when they sang "What Makes You Special, Canadian Child?".
Aunt T cried, too.

Here we are, singing "O Canada." Mr. Nguyen was louder than the bagpipes. He sure could *sing* English!

We had a reception in the library. Everyone was very happy. We ate tiny sandwiches. Sophia and Maria and I liked the round ones made with bread, Cheese Whiz, and a sweet pickle rolled up inside. There were lots of cakes and cookies, too.

In the afternoon Mama and Baba went back to work and I went back to my class. Everyone was happy for me. Ms. Fox presented me with a little gift. Inside the box was a tiny Canadian flag pin. I loved the way it sparkled. At recess we built a snowman.

The biggest surprise happened at supper time. I was setting the table for Mama, Baba, and me. In walked Aunt T and Uncle Doug and my cousins carrying food. The DeSantis family from next door arrived with a giant pan of lasagne and garlic bread.

More friends and neighbours came. John, from the restaurant where Baba works, showed up with plates and knives and forks and glasses, and Greek ribs. His family came, too. Soon the house was full and the kitchen was filled with food. I ate so many perogies I thought I'd burst. Ms. Fox brought home-made chocolates in the shape of maple leaves. They were delicious. It was a wonderful day.

I fell asleep with my lucky red shoes on.

TO BE A

Before the Canadian Citizenship Act was passed, people who lived in Canada were considered to be British subjects. This changed because of the efforts of the Honourable Paul Martin, Sr. Near the end of World War II, while visiting a Canadian military cemetery in France, he saw the sacrifice made by young men from all across Canada. He wanted to honour their memory as well as have Canada recognized for its contribution to world peace. With the support of Prime Minister William Lyon Mackenzie King, the Canadian Citizenship Act came into effect on January 1, 1947. The current Act was passed in 1977, whereby citizenship can be acquired only by birth in Canada, or by having a Canadian parent, or by making legal application (naturalization).

O CANADA

O Canada!

Our home and native land!

True patriot love in all thy sons command.

With glowing hearts, we see thee rise,

The True North strong and free!

From far and wide, O Canada,

We stand on guard for thee.

God keep our land glorious and free!

O Canada, we stand on guard for thee.

O Canada, we stand on guard for thee.

O Canada!

Terre de nos aïeux,

Ton front est ceint de fleurons glorieux!

Car ton bras sait porter l'épée

Il sait porter la croix!

Ton histoire est une épopée

Des plus brillants exploits.

Et ta valeur, de foi trempée,

Protégera nos foyers et nos droits.

Protégera nos foyers et nos droits.

CANADIAN

To apply for Canadian citizenship, you must:
- Be 18 years of age or older;
- Be a permanent resident who was lawfully admitted to Canada;
- Have lived here for three of the previous four years;
- Speak either English or French;
- Pass a written test that asks questions about voting, Canadian history, geography, government, and the rights and responsibilities of Canadian citizens.

The citizenship ceremony is the final step in becoming a Canadian citizen. At the ceremony you must take the Oath of Citizenship and sign the Oath form. All ceremonies end with the singing of Canada's national anthem, "O Canada."

As a Canadian citizen you are entitled to:
- Vote in federal and provincial / territorial elections;
- Be a candidate in federal and provincial / territorial elections;
- Learn in either official language;
- Enter and leave Canada freely;
- Perform jury duty;
- Apply for a Canadian passport.

The passport is a little blue booklet that requests the bearer's safe passage in the name of Her Majesty the Queen. The governor general, the prime minister of Canada, the lieutenant governors, and our diplomats have red passports. Special green passports are used by members of parliament, senators, and premiers when representing Canada abroad.

As Canadian citizens, we share the responsibility to:
- Vote in elections;
- Obey Canada's laws;
- Work to help others in the community;
- Care for Canada's heritage;
- Express opinions freely while respecting the rights and freedoms of others;
- Eliminate discrimination and injustice.

The author and the publisher acknowledge the help and cooperation of Citizenship and Immigration Canada in granting permission for use of information contained in *A Look at Canada* © Minister of Government Services Canada 1995.

"Very few Canadians share a common past, but all of us share a common future."

Dr. Robert Williamson